D1252454

Clouds

Andrea Rivera

abdopublishing.com

Published by Abdo Zoom™, PO Box 398166, Minneapolis, Minnesota 55439. Copyright © 2017 by Abdo Consulting Group, Inc. International copyrights reserved in all countries. No part of this book may be reproduced in any form without written permission from the publisher. Abdo Zoom™ is a trademark and logo of Abdo Consulting Group, Inc.

Printed in the United States of America, North Mankato, Minnesota
102016
012017

THIS BOOK CONTAINS RECYCLED MATERIALS

Cover Photo: Shutterstock Images
Interior Photos: Shutterstock Images, 1, 6, 6–7; Datskevich Aleh/Shutterstock Images, 5; NASA, 8, 9; W. L. Davies/ iStockphoto, 10; Alberto Pomares/iStockphoto, 11; John Kirk/iStockphoto, 12–13; Brian A. Jackson/ Shutterstock Images, 14; S. Borisov/Shutterstock Images, 15; UK Art Photo/Alamy, 17; iStockphoto, 18, 19; Jaya Kumar/Shutterstock Images, 21

Editor: Emily Temple
Series Designer: Madeline Berger
Art Direction: Dorothy Toth

Publisher's Cataloging-in-Publication Data
Names: Rivera, Andrea, author.
Title: Clouds / by Andrea Rivera.
Description: Minneapolis, MN : Abdo Zoom, 2017. | Series: In the sky |
    Includes bibliographical references and index.
Identifiers: LCCN 2016948918 | ISBN 9781680799316 (lib. bdg.) |
    ISBN 9781624025174 (ebook) | ISBN 9781624025730 (Read-to-me ebook)
Subjects: LCSH: Clouds--Juvenile literature.
Classification: DDC 551.57/6--dc23
LC record available at http://lccn.loc.gov/2016948918

Table of Contents

Clouds are made of water and air. The sun's heat turns water into **vapor**. Vapor rises into the sky.

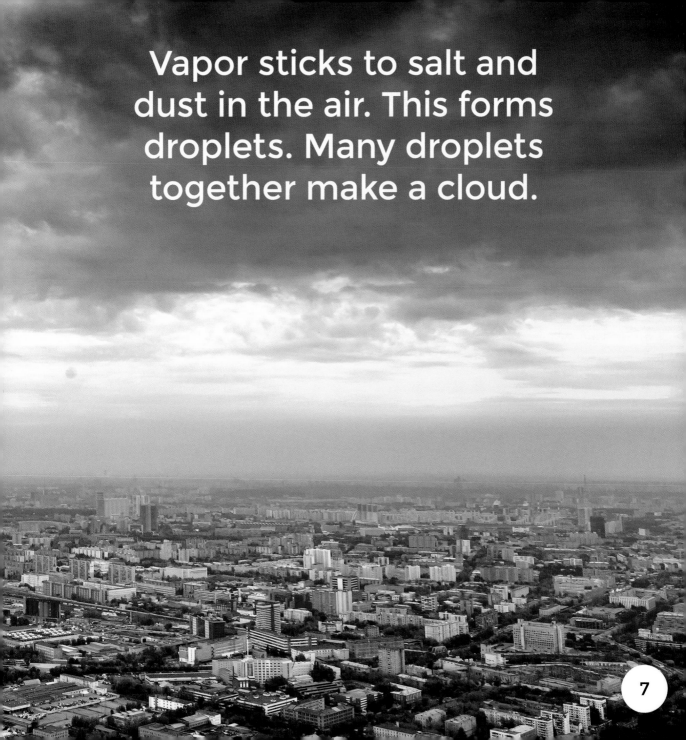

Vapor sticks to salt and dust in the air. This forms droplets. Many droplets together make a cloud.

Technology

Satellites track clouds. They show how the clouds move.

This helps scientists find wind speed. They can **predict** the weather.

Cloud shapes help predict the weather, too. **Stratus clouds** bring rain or snow.

Cirrus clouds mean the weather will change.

Cloud seeding could force clouds to rain.

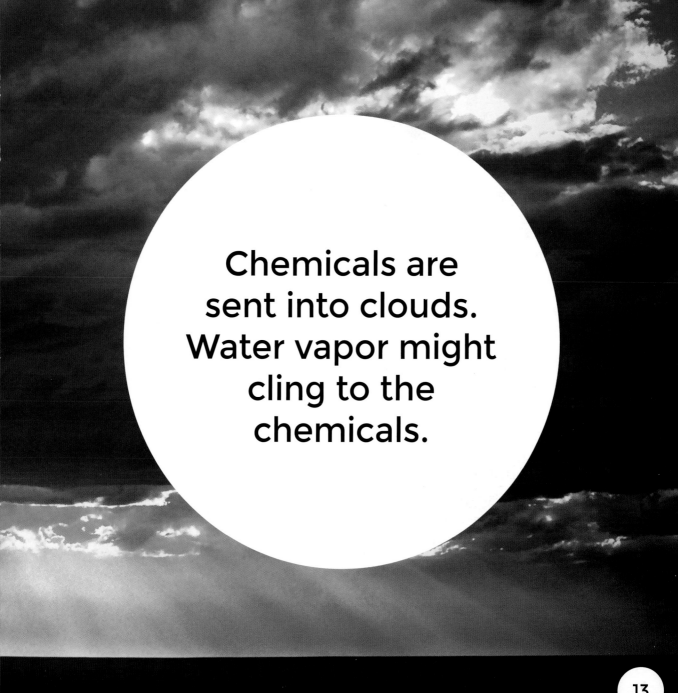

Chemicals are sent into clouds. Water vapor might cling to the chemicals.

This might form raindrops.

However, scientists are not certain if cloud seeding works.

Art

One artist makes clouds indoors.
He uses a smoke machine.
He sprays water in the air.
The water sticks to the smoke.

A cloud forms.

17

Math

Clouds are grouped by their height. Low clouds are less than 6,500 feet (2,000 m) from the ground.

High clouds are at least 16,500 feet (5,000 m) above the ground.

Key Stats

- Clouds are made of water and air. White clouds are more air than water. Dark clouds are more water than air.

- Clouds can travel through the sky at 100 miles per hour (160 km/h).

- Cumulonimbus clouds are big, dark storm clouds. They can grow to be 60,000 feet (18,300 m) tall. That is more than 11 miles (17.7 km).

Glossary

cirrus cloud - a high, thin cloud that forms wispy white bands.

cloud seeding - sending chemicals into clouds to make rain.

predict - to guess what might happen in the future.

satellite - a device that orbits the earth.

stratus cloud - a low, gray cloud that usually forms flat layers.

vapor - very tiny drops of water that float in the air.

Booklinks

For more information
on clouds, please visit
booklinks.abdopublishing.com

 In on STEAM!

Learn even more with the Abdo Zoom
STEAM database. Check out
abdozoom.com for more information.

Index